WonderWorks

Decodable Reader

Unit 4

Mc Graw Hill

Contents

A Good Ride in Bug's Brook
Winston Trudeau
illustrated by Kersti Frigell
1

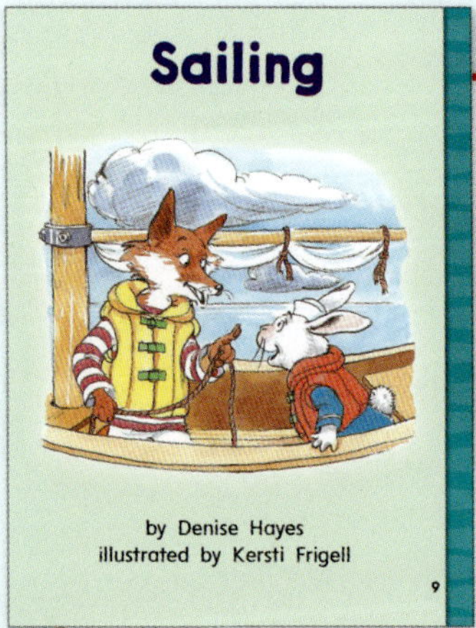
Sailing
by Denise Hayes
illustrated by Kersti Frigell
9

East Side Beach
by Olinda Smith
illustrated by Kristen Goeters
17

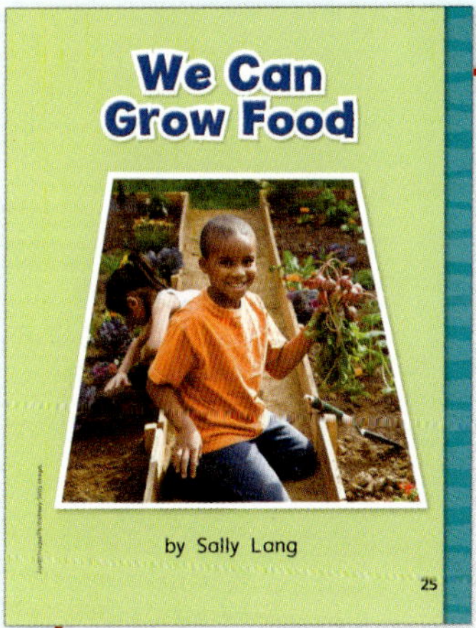
We Can Grow Food
by Sally Lang
25

Let's Find Dwight!
by Jamie Cydzik
illustrated by Linda Bleck
33

A Good Ride in Bug's Brook

Winston Trudeau
illustrated by Kersti Frigell

Bug lived alone by a brook. She liked jumping in this brook and riding. **Every** ride Bug took felt like fun.

Bug was **done** with **work** on this day. She dipped a foot in and skimmed along.

Then she sat up quick.
Bug's brook was rushing fast.
Bug stood up. The brook was racing.

Soon Bug's brook went past a crooked bend.

Bug stood shaking at the top.
Can Bug get down and not
slip in this racing brook?

Bug felt fine **after** this ride.
Bug said, “I will **buy** a
helmet for the next ride.”

Sailing

by Denise Hayes
illustrated by Kersti Frigell

Ray hopes it does not rain.
He runs on the wooden dock.
Jay is waiting for him.
It is after **eight**.

This little sailing ship will **carry** the two **animals**. Jay tells Ray, "It is **about** to rain. Let's wait a while."

Ray states, “I’m not afraid of rain. Let’s go.”

Jay explains, “Let’s stay safe. I will check this sail.”

"Sails have names. This sail is the main," Jay tells Ray.

"When will we sail on **our** way?" asks Ray.

Ray grabs the rope. Just then, rain drips on the ship. "Wait, Ray! Let's **give** up! It is raining," yells Jay.

Jay picks up Ray. “Let’s wait for the next nice day.”

Ray states, “That is a shame, but I will wait.”

East Side Beach

by Olinda Smith
illustrated by Kristen Goeters

Jean and Dean sit on steps.
The kids feel the heat.
It is hot **because** the sun is
beating down.

Mom asks, "Will we sit in the shade **or** ride to the Beach?"

Jean and Dean agree, "Let's ride to East Side Beach!"

Mom plans the trip.
They stop to eat.
East Side Beach is on the
other side of the state line.

At last, they reach the beach.
They see and smell the sea.
Sea breezes sweep in.
They can't wait to swim.

Mom takes a brief dip. Then she reads. Jean and Dean step **into** the **blue** sea. Dean fills and refills a **small** pail.

"Can we stay late?" asks Jean.

Mom smiles. "Yes, we can."

Jean and Dean play till the sun sets!

We Can Grow Food

Jupiterimages/Photolibrary/Getty Images

by Sally Lang

moodboard/Cultura/Getty Images

Cultura/SuperStock

We hope to grow food.
Where should we **start**?
We locate a nice plot.
Then, we dig with hoes.

Cultura Creative/Alamy

Next, we plant seeds in rows.
We soak them with water.

The sun keeps them **warm**.
Green plants begin growing.

Alistair Berg/Digital Vision/Getty Images

When we **find** weeds, we pull them up.

Our goal is to make growing space for good plants.

©Tim Pannell/Corbis

These plants grow and grow. We add stakes to hold them up. We brush bugs off so they will not eat the plants.

Jupiterimages/Photolibrary/Getty Images

Soon growing time is **over**.

It is time for picking. We pick a lot of **food** in our own plot.

We load the food in bins. We have **more** than we need.

We will donate this food to those who need it.

Let's Find Dwight!

by Jamie Cydzik
illustrated by Linda Bleck

“Hi Joe!” said Gail. “What’s going on?”

“I might cry. I can’t find my pet Dwight,” said Joe.

"I think I **know** where he went," said Gail.
"He flew by me. This way!"

Gail and Joe ran to the trees. But Dwight was not in sight. Joe sighed.

"Listen," said Gail. *Tweet, tweet, tweet.*

The tweets **were** up high.

Joe and Gail looked up.

"Dwight!" cried Joe. "He is shy. How can we get him?" Mom had grapes in her bag. "I can try. A snack might coax him down."

Dwight **flew** to them. Gail **caught** him.

Dwight tweeted his thanks.

Gail and Joe **laugh**, "We got you, Dwight!"

Unit 4

Word Count: 97

Decodable Words

Target Phonics Element: Variant Vowel /ů/: *oo*
brook, crooked, foot, stood, took
Review: *a, and, alone, along, at, bends, Bug, Bug's, but, can, did, dipped, fast, felt, fine, fun, get, had, helmet, I, in, it, jumping, like, liked, next, not, on, past, plans, quick, racing, ride, riding, rushed, rushing, sat, shaking, skimmed, slip, then, this, top, up, use, went, will, with*

High-Frequency Words

after, buy, done, every, soon, work
Review: *by, day, down, lived, my, she, the, to, too, very, was*

Word Count: 124

Decodable Words

Target Phonics Element: Long *a (ai, ay)*
afraid, explains, Jay, main, rain, raining, Ray, sail, sails, sailing, stay, wait, waiting, way
Review: *a, asks, but, check, day, dock, drips, grabs, him, hopes, I, I'm, is, it, just, let's, names, next, nice, not, on, picks, rope, runs, safe, shame, ship, states, tells, that, then, this, up, when, while, will, wooden, yells*

High-Frequency Words

about, animal, carry, eight, give, our
Review: *after, does, for, go, have, he, little, of, the, to, two, we*

Week 3 • *East Side Beach* .... page 17

Word Count: 129

Decodable Words

Target Phonics Element: Long *e (e, ee, ea, ie)*
agree, beach, beating, breezes, brief, Dean, east, eat, feel, heat, Jean, reach, reads, sea, sweep, we
Review: *a, and, asks, at, can, can't, dip, fills, hot, in, is, it, kids, last, late, let's, line, Mom, on, pail, plans, play, refills, ride, set, shade, side, sit, smell, smiles, state, stay, see, she, step, steps, stop, sun, swim, takes, the, then, till, trip, wait, will, yes*

High-Frequency Words

because, blue, into, or, other, small
Review: *down, of, they, to, we*

Week 4 • *We Can Grow Food*.................... page 25

Word Count: 131

Decodable Words

Target Phonics Element: Long *o (o, oa, ow, oe)*
donate, goal, grow, growing, hoes, hold, load, locate, own, so, soak, rows
Review: *a, add, and, begin, big, bins, brush, can, dig, eat, end, green, hope, in, is, it, keeps, long, lots, make, need, next, nice, off, pick, picking, plant, plants, plot, seeds, space, stakes, sun, than, the, them, then, these, this, those, time, up, we, weeds, when, will, with*

High-Frequency Words

find, food, more, over, start, warm
Review: *for, of, our, pull, should, soon, they, to, water, where, who*

Week 5 • *Let's Find Dwight!* .... page 33

Word Count: 111

Decodable Words

Target Phonics Element: Long *i (i, y, igh, ie)*
by, cried, cry, Dwight, find, hi, high, I, might, my, shy, sighed, sight, tight, try
Review: *bag, but, can, can't, coax, had, he, him, Gail, get, grapes, going, in, Joe, me, Mom, not, on, pet, ran, snack, think, this, trees, tweet, up, went, way, we*

High-Frequency Words

caught, flew, know, laugh, listen, were
Review: *are, down, looked, said, so, the, to, you, where*

Decoding skills taught to date:

Phonics: Consonants/Letter Recognition; Short *a*; Short *i*; *l*-Blends; Short *o*; *r*-Blends, *s*-Blends; Short *e (e, ea)*; Short *u*; End Blends *nd, nk, nt, st, sk, mp*; Consonant Digraphs: *th, sh, -ng*; Consonant Digraphs *ch, -tch, wh, ph*; Long *a (a_e)*; Long *i (i_e)*; Soft *c*; Soft *g, dge*; Long *o (o_e)*; Long *u (u_e)*; Long *e (e_e)*; Variant Vowel /u̇/: *oo, u*; Long *a (a, ai, ay)*; Long *e (e, ee, ea, ie)*; Long *o (o, oa, ow, oe)*; Long *i (i, y, igh, ie)*

Structural Analysis: Consonants; Inflectional Ending *-s* (plurals, verbs); Double Final Consonants; Alphabetical Order; Possessives with *'s*; Inflectional Ending *-ed*; Contractions with *'s*; Inflectional Ending *-ing*; Closed Syllables; Inflectional Ending *-es*; Contractions with *n't*; Plurals with CVC*e* Words; Inflectional Endings *-ed, -ing* with Spelling Changes; CVC*e* Syllables; Inflectional Endings *-ed, -ing* Double Final Consonant; Alphabetical Order (two letters); Prefixes *re-, un-, pre-*; Open Syllables; Inflectional Endings Change *y* to *i*